A QUESTRON™ ELECTRONIC   T5-AOK-730

MY FIRST BOOK OF SUBTRACTION

QUESTRON™

PRICE/STERN/SLOAN
Publishers, Inc., Los Angeles

DISTRIBUTED BY
RANDOM HOUSE, INC.
New York

THE QUESTRON™ SYSTEM
COMBINING FUN WITH LEARNING

This book is part of **THE QUESTRON SYSTEM**, which offers children a unique aid to learning and endless hours of challenging entertainment.

The QUESTRON electronic "wand" uses a microchip to sense correct and incorrect answers with "right" or "wrong" sounds and lights. Victory sounds and lights reward the user when particular sets of questions or games are completed. Powered by a nine-volt alkaline battery, which is activated only when the wand is pressed on a page, QUESTRON should have an exceptionally long life. The QUESTRON ELECTRONIC WAND can be used with any book in the QUESTRON series.

A note to parents...

With QUESTRON, right or wrong answers are indicated instantly and can be tried over and over to reinforce learning and improve skills. Children need not be restricted to the books designated for their age group, as interests and rates of development vary widely. Also, within many of the books, certain pages are designed for the older end of the age group and will provide a stimulating challenge to younger children.

Many activities are designed at different levels. For example, the child can select an answer by recognizing a letter or by reading an entire word. The activities for pre-readers and early readers are intended to be used with parental assistance. Interaction with parents or older children will stimulate the learning experience.

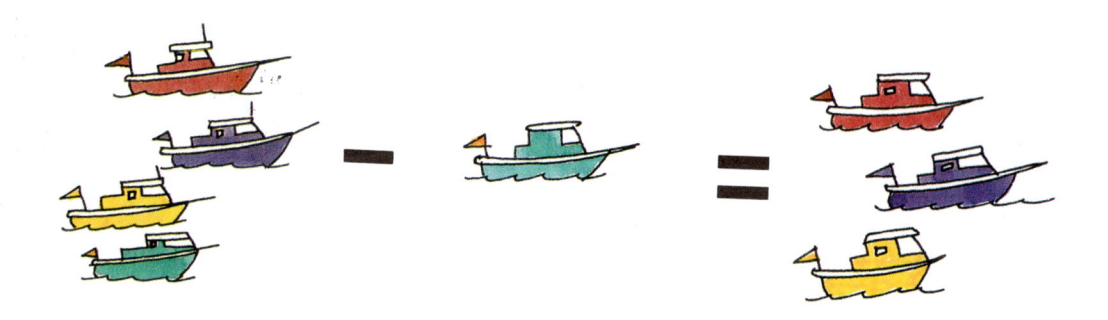

QUESTRON Project Director: Roger Burrows
Editorial Coordinators/Art Directors: Judy Walker, Lee A. Scott
Writer: Beverley Dietz
Illustrator Kathleen McCarthy
Editor: Susan Cohn

Copyright ©1986 by Price/Stern/Sloan Publishers, Inc. All rights reserved under International and Pan-American Copyright Conventions. No part of this publication may be reproduced, stored in a retrieval system, or transmitted in any form or by any means, electronic, mechanical, photocopying, recording or otherwise, without the prior written permission of the publisher. Published by Price/Stern/Sloan Publishers, Inc., 410 North La Cienega Boulevard, Los Angeles, California 90048. Distributed by Random House, Inc., 201 East 50th Street, New York, New York 10022. ISBN: 0-394-88172-9
1 2 3 4 5 6 7 8 9 0

QUESTRON™ is a trademark of Price/Stern/Sloan Publishers, Inc.
U.S.A. and International Patents Pending
Manufactured in the U.S.A.

HOW TO START QUESTRON

Hold **QUESTRON** at this angle and press the activator button firmly on the page.

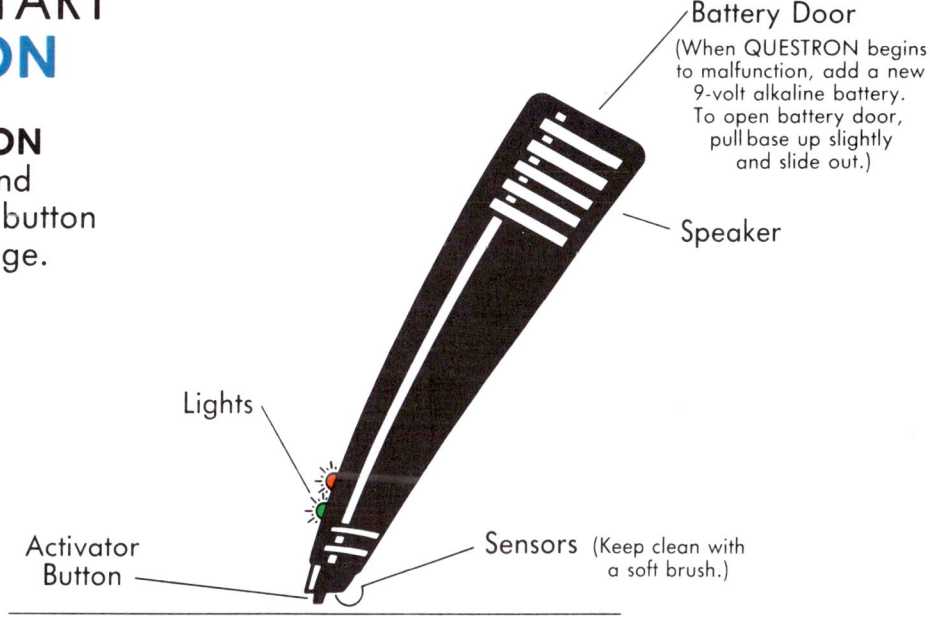

- Battery Door (When QUESTRON begins to malfunction, add a new 9-volt alkaline battery. To open battery door, pull base up slightly and slide out.)
- Speaker
- Lights
- Activator Button
- Sensors (Keep clean with a soft brush.)

HOW TO USE QUESTRON

PRESS
Press **QUESTRON** firmly on the shape below, then lift it off.

TRACK
Press **QUESTRON** down on "Start" and keep it pressed down as you move to "Finish."

RIGHT & WRONG WITH QUESTRON

Press **QUESTRON** on the square.

Press **QUESTRON** on the circle.

Press **QUESTRON** on the triangle.

See the green light and hear the sound. This green light and sound say "You are correct."

Hear the victory sound. Don't be dazzled by the flashing lights. You deserve them.

The red light and sound say "Try again." Lift **QUESTRON** off the page and wait for the sound to stop.

It's Magic

Solve each subtraction problem.
Press **Questron** on the correct answer box.

Skill: Subtracting from 2 and 1

Circus Parade

Solve each subtraction problem.
Press **Questron** on the correct answer box.

Skill: Subtracting from 3

5

At the Beach

Look at the pictures in each box. Press **Questron** on the number sentence which matches the pictures.

$2 - 1 = 3$
$2 - 1 = 1$
$3 + 1 = 1$

$1 + 1 = 2$
$1 - 1 = 2$
$2 - 1 = 2$

$3 - 1 = 1$
$3 - 2 = 1$
$3 + 1 = 2$

Skill: Reviewing subtraction and addition facts — numbers 1 to 3

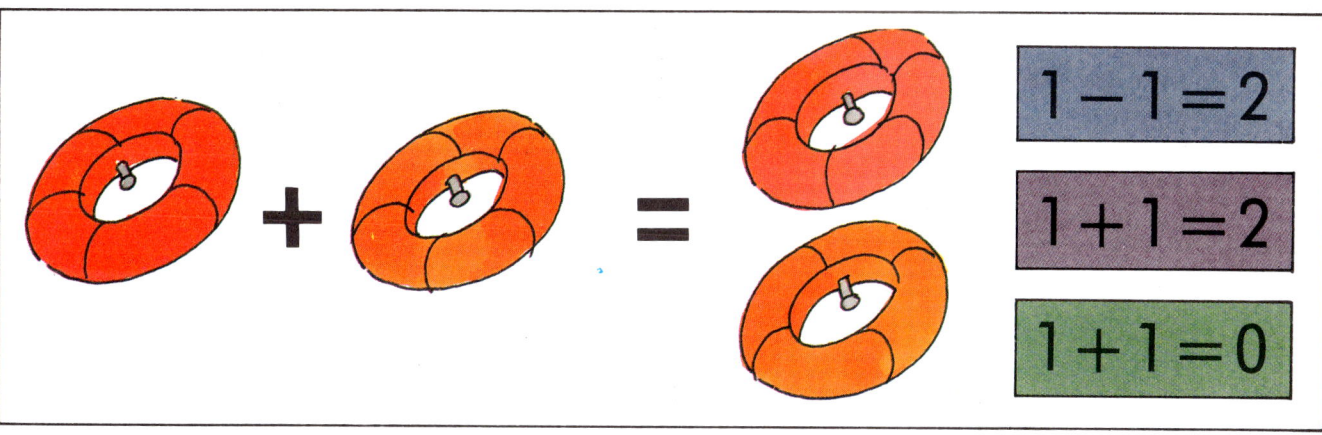

$1-1=2$

$1+1=2$

$1+1=0$

$2-1=0$

$2-2=0$

$2+1=2$

$3+1=3$

$3-2=2$

$3-0=3$

Setting Sail

Solve each subtraction problem.
Press **Questron** on the correct answer box.

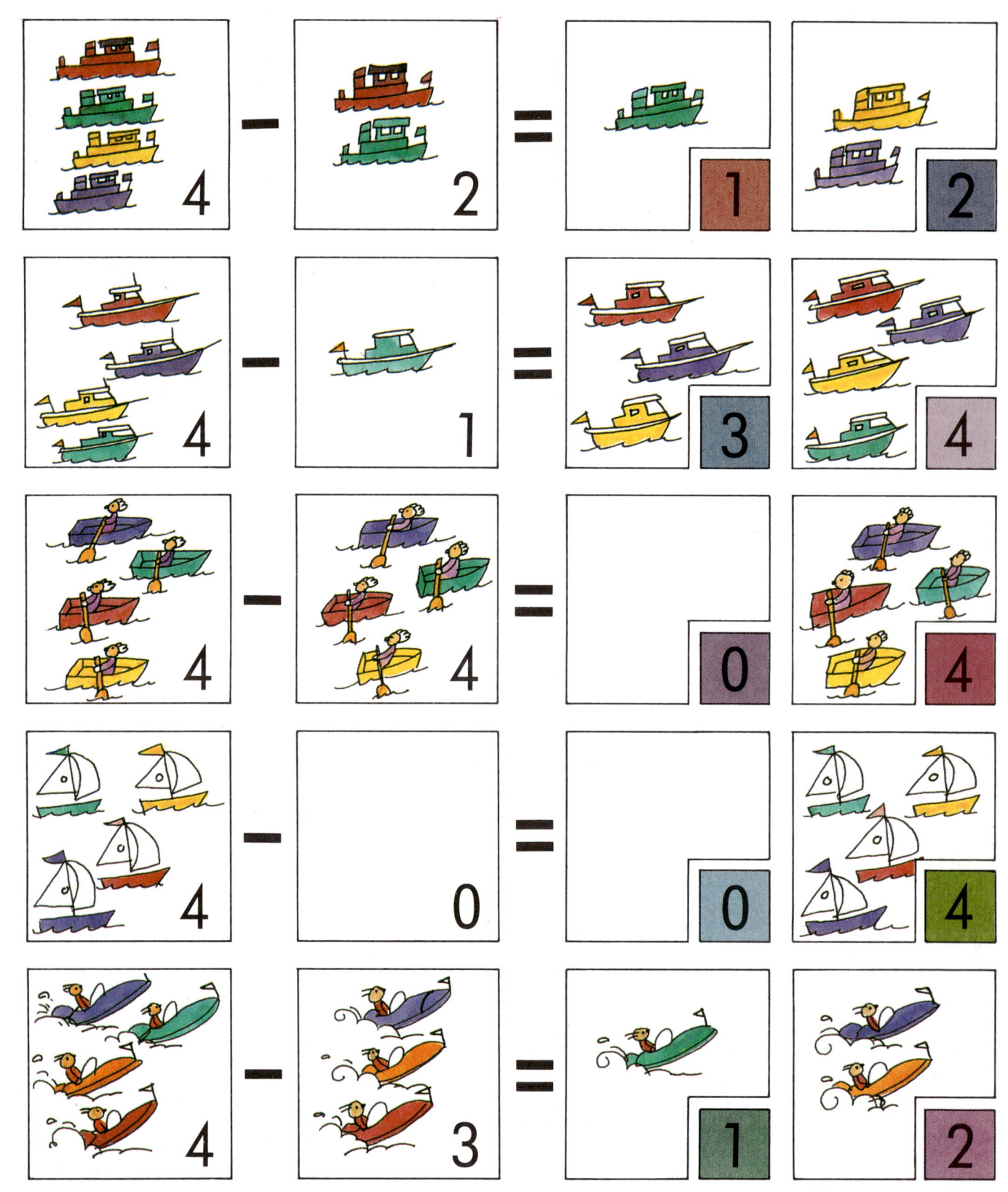

4	− 2	=	1	2
4	− 1	=	3	4
4	− 4	=	0	4
4	− 0	=	0	4
4	− 3	=	1	2

Skill: Subtracting from 4

They're Off

Solve each subtraction problem.
Press **Questron** on the correct answer box.

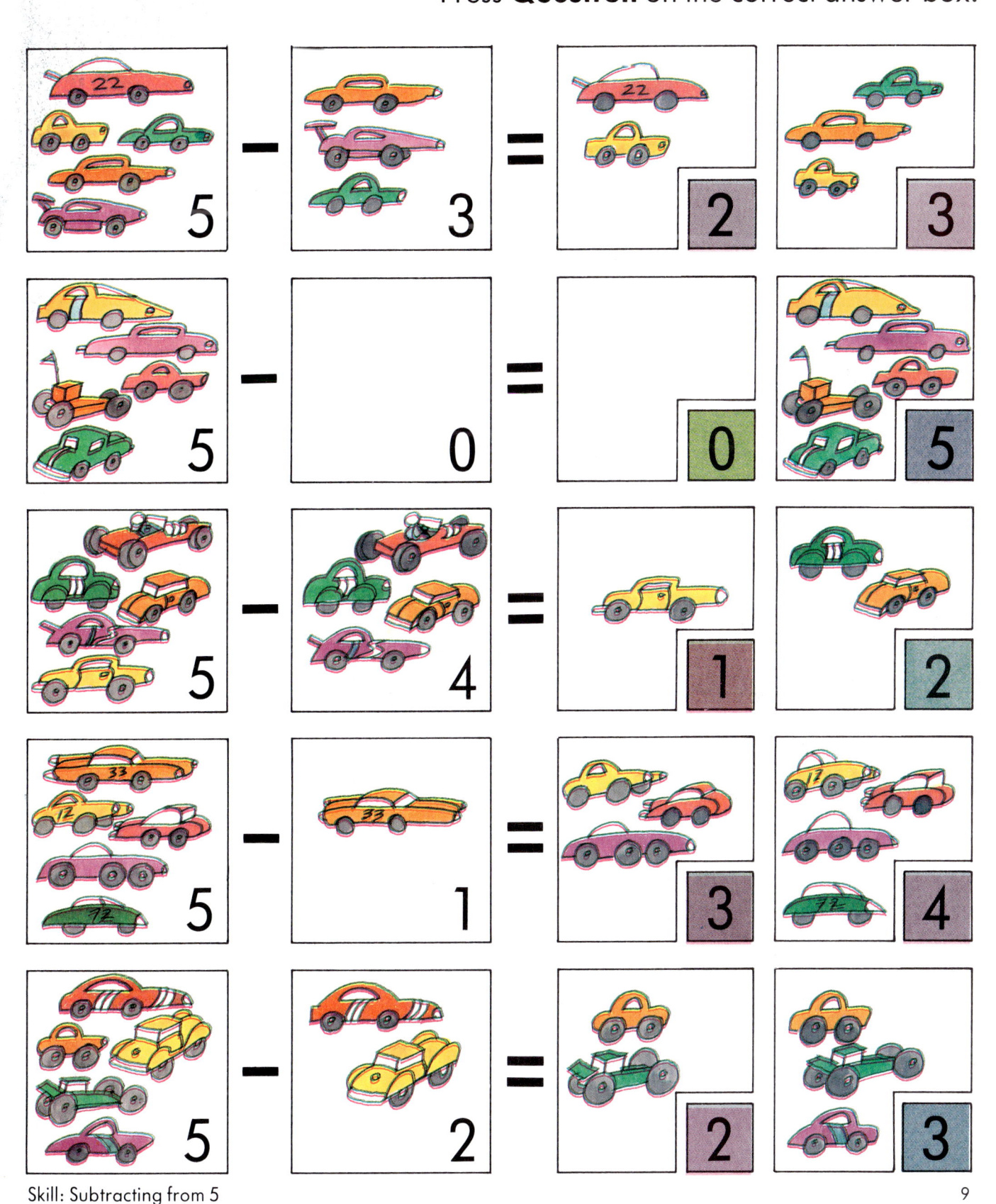

5 − 3 = 2 | 3

5 − 0 = 0 | 5

5 − 4 = 1 | 2

5 − 1 = 3 | 4

5 − 2 = 2 | 3

Skill: Subtracting from 5

Sliding Down

Solve the puzzle at the top of each slide. If the answer is **2**, track **Questron** to the number **2**. Start on the ☆.

2+1 ☆

5−3 ☆

3−1 ☆

1+1 ☆

2−0 ☆

4−3 ☆

2

Skill: Reviewing subtraction and addition facts — numbers 1 to 5

Climbing Ladders

Solve the puzzle at the bottom of each ladder. If the answer is **3**, track **Questron** to the number **3**. Start on the ☆.

3

3−0

4−1

0+3

5−2

2+1

1+3

Skill: Reviewing subtraction and addition facts — numbers 1 to 5

For Sale

Press **Questron** on the correct answer boxes.

The store had 2 . 
0 were sold.
How many are left?
| 0 | 1 | 2 |

The store had 3 . 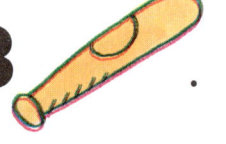
2 were sold.
How many are left?
| 1 | 3 | 5 |

The store had 1 .
1 was sold.
How many are left?
| 0 | 1 | 2 |

The store had 5 . 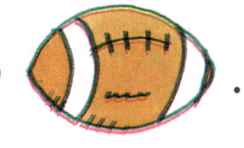
3 were sold.
How many are left?
| 1 | 2 | 3 |

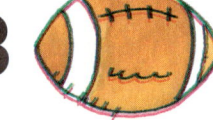

Skill: Solving word problems with subtraction

The store had 3 🛹.

3 🛹 were sold.

How many are left?

| 0 | 3 | 6 |

The store had 4 🚲.

3 🚲 were sold.

How many are left?

| 1 | 3 | 5 |

The store had 4 🧤.

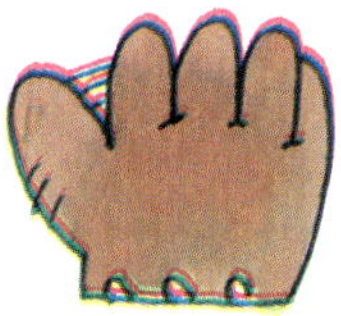

1 🧤 was sold.

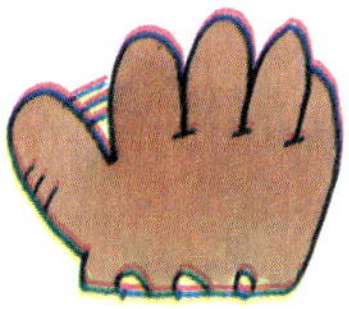

How many are left?

| 1 | 3 | 5 |

The store had 5 ⚽.

5 ⚽ were sold.

How many are left?

| 0 | 1 | 2 |

13

Planting a Garden

Press **Questron** on the correct answer boxes.

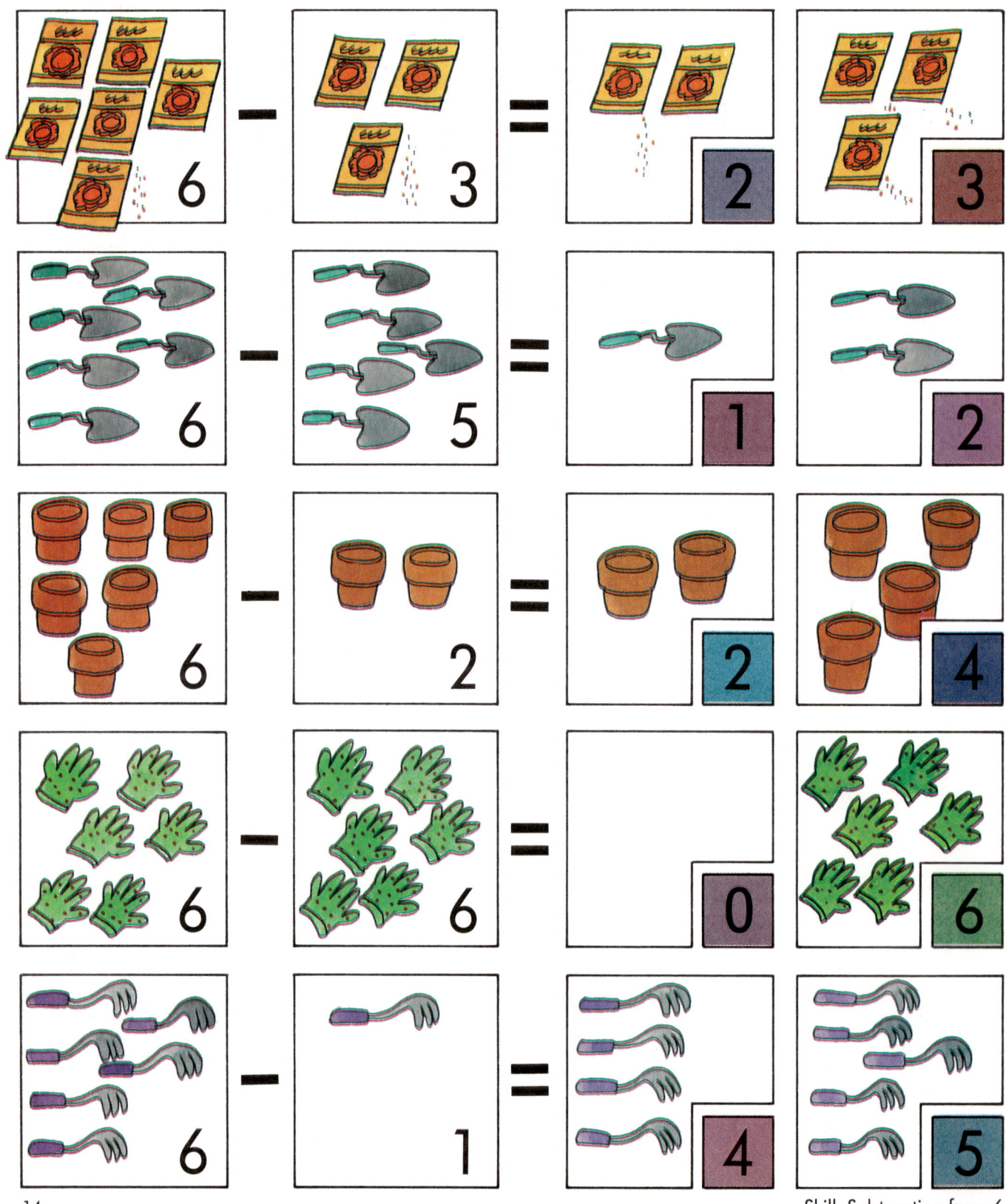

6 − 3 = 2 / 3

6 − 5 = 1 / 2

6 − 2 = 2 / 4

6 − 6 = 0 / 6

6 − 1 = 4 / 5

Skill: Subtracting from 6

Growing a Garden

Press **Questron** on the correct answer boxes.

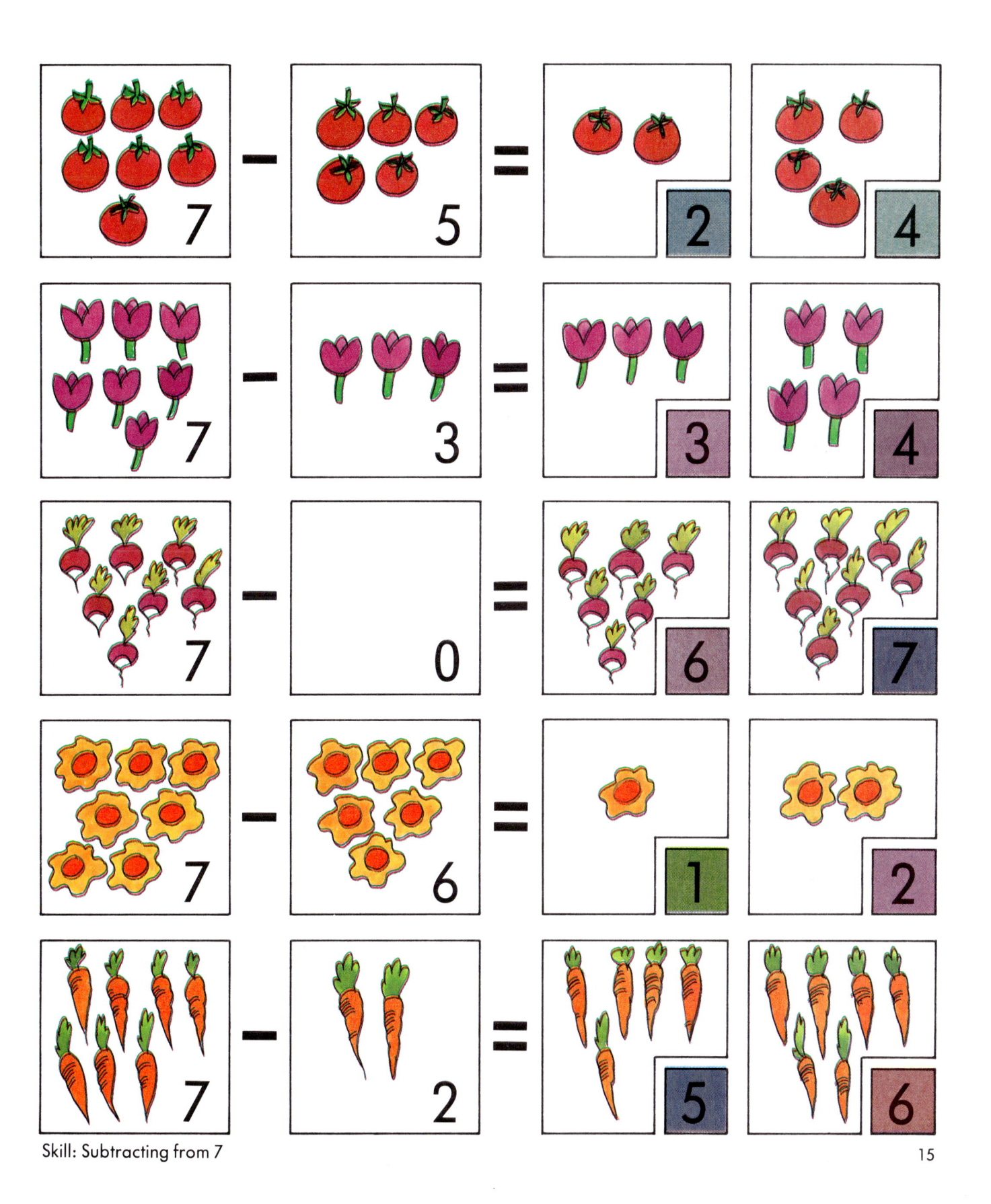

Skill: Subtracting from 7

Time Trials

Track **Questron** on the path that has the correct answers.
Start on the ☆.

$4-3=$

$5-4=$ $5-3=$

$4-2=$ $2-2=$

Skill: Completing correct number sentences

3−1=
4−4=
5−0=
3−2=
1−0=

Gone Fishing

Look at the number on each boat.
Which number sentences does it finish?
Press **Questron** on the correct fish.

6
- 7−1=
- 4+2=
- 5−1=

2
- 6−5=
- 5−3=
- 2+0=

1
- 7−6=
- 1−0=
- 6−5=

4
- 5−1=
- 7−4=
- 6−2=

Skill: Reviewing subtraction and addition facts — numbers 1 to 7

3
5+2=
6−3=
7−4=

7
7−0=
3+4=
6+1=

0
3+3=
3−3=
6−6=

5
5−1=
1−2=
3+2=

Busy Bugs

Press **Questron** on the correct answer boxes.

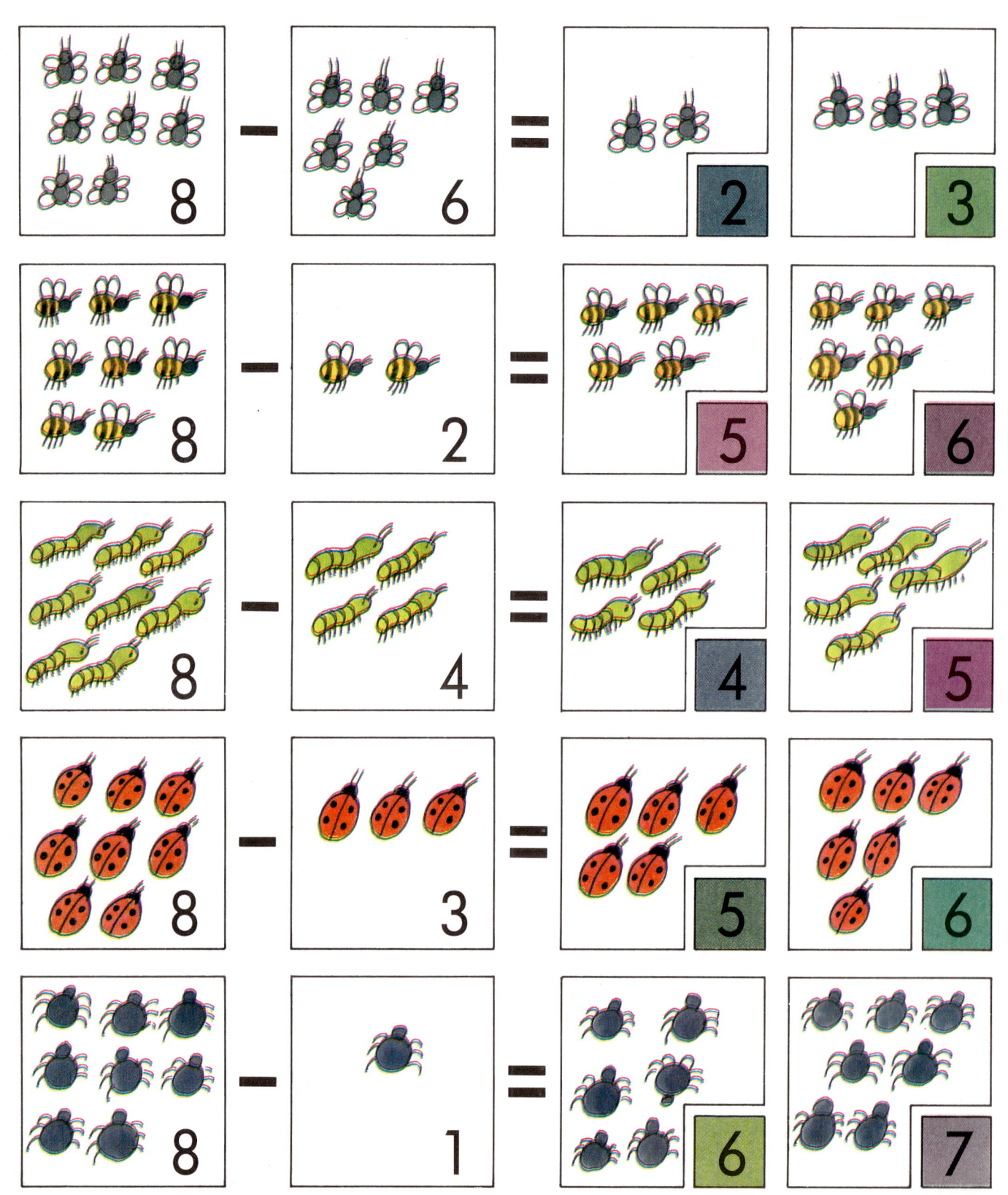

8 − 6 = 2 | 3

8 − 2 = 5 | 6

8 − 4 = 4 | 5

8 − 3 = 5 | 6

8 − 1 = 6 | 7

Skill: Subtracting from 8

Bug Bonanza

Press **Questron** on the correct answer boxes.

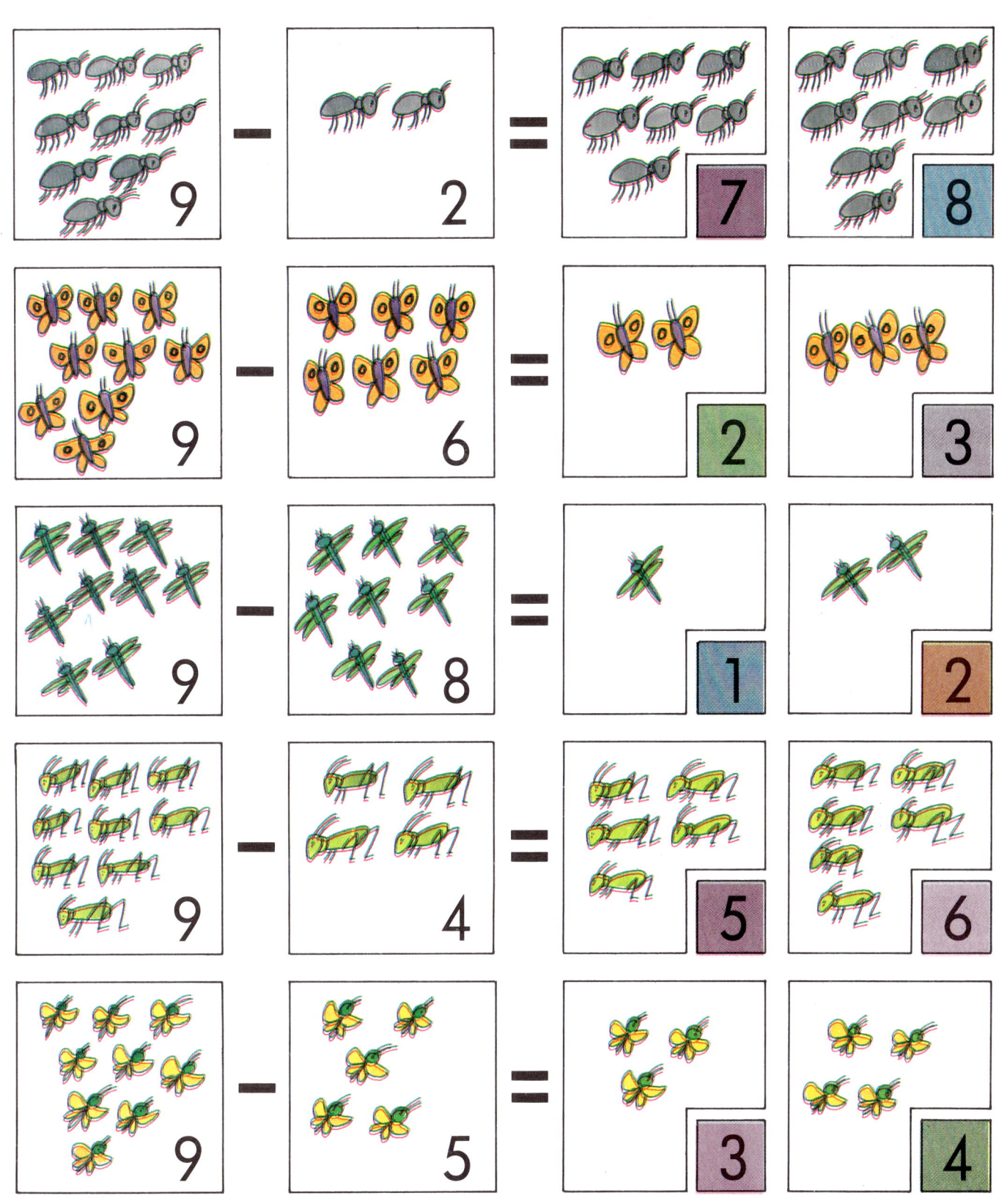

9	− 2	=	7	8
9	− 6	=	2	3
9	− 8	=	1	2
9	− 4	=	5	6
9	− 5	=	3	4

Skill: Subtracting from 9

Fly Away

Press **Questron** on the correct answer boxes.

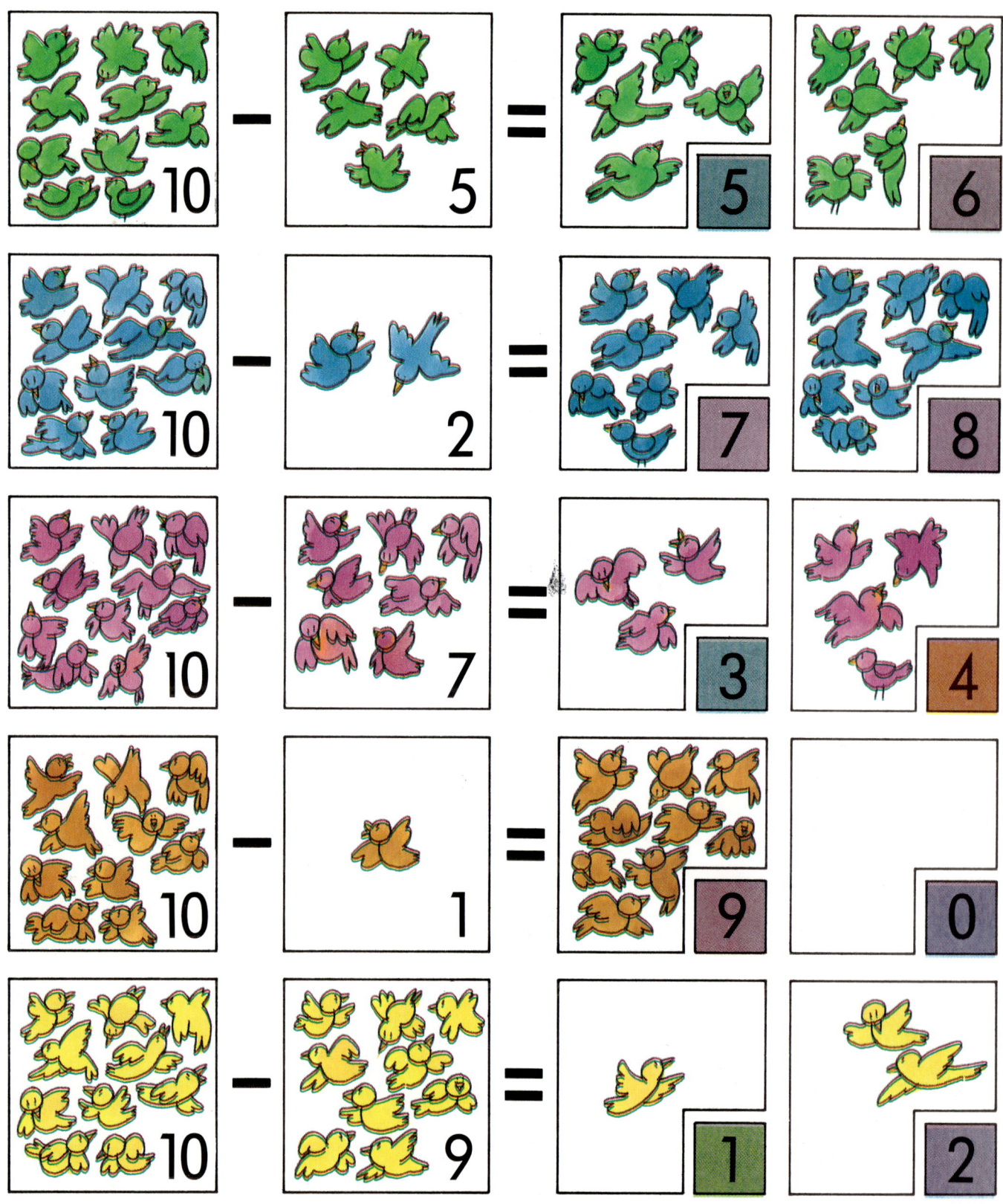

10	−	5	=	5	6
10	−	2	=	7	8
10	−	7	=	3	4
10	−	1	=	9	0
10	−	9	=	1	2

Skill: Subtracting from 10

10 − 4 = 4 | 6

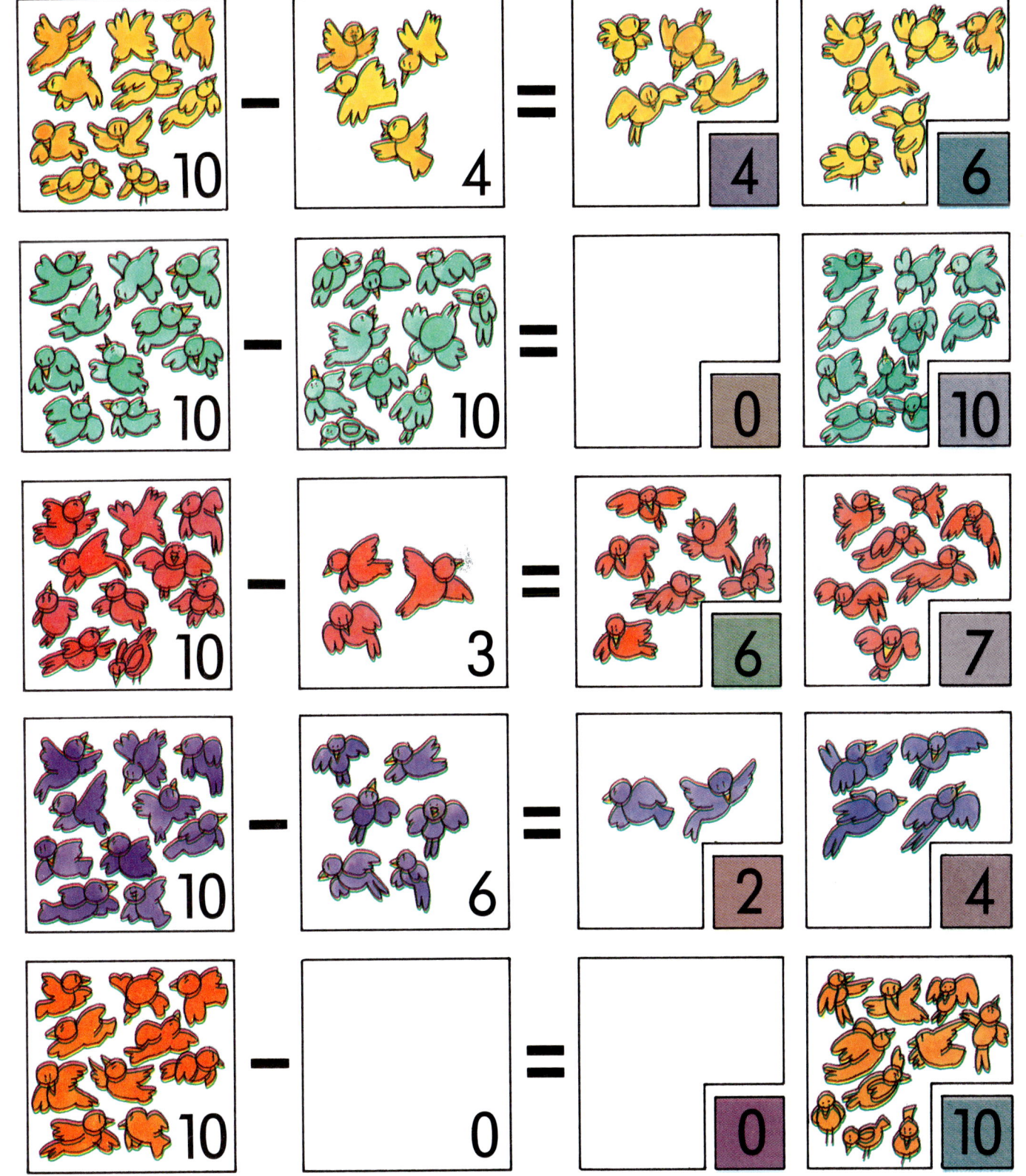

10 − 10 = 0 | 10

10 − 3 = 6 | 7

10 − 6 = 2 | 4

10 − 0 = 0 | 10

Fancy Footwork

Track **Questron** on the path that has the problems with correct answers. Start on the ☆.

$$\begin{array}{r}4\\-2\\\hline 1\end{array}$$

$$\begin{array}{r}7\\-4\\\hline 2\end{array}$$

$$\begin{array}{r}4\\-2\\\hline 2\end{array}$$

$$\begin{array}{r}7\\-4\\\hline 3\end{array}$$

$$\begin{array}{r}6\\-3\\\hline 3\end{array}$$

$$\begin{array}{r}6\\-3\\\hline 2\end{array}$$

$$\begin{array}{r}8\\-5\\\hline 3\end{array}$$

$$\begin{array}{r}10\\-3\\\hline 8\end{array}$$

$$\begin{array}{r}8\\-5\\\hline 4\end{array}$$

$$\begin{array}{r}10\\-3\\\hline 7\end{array}$$

Skill: Identifying correct subtraction problems

$$\begin{array}{r}5\\-4\\\hline 2\end{array}$$

$$\begin{array}{r}1\\-0\\\hline 1\end{array}$$

$$\begin{array}{r}5\\-4\\\hline 1\end{array}$$

$$\begin{array}{r}1\\-0\\\hline 0\end{array}$$

$$\begin{array}{r}9\\-6\\\hline 3\end{array}$$

$$\begin{array}{r}9\\-6\\\hline 2\end{array}$$

$$\begin{array}{r}3\\-1\\\hline 4\end{array}$$

$$\begin{array}{r}2\\-2\\\hline 0\end{array}$$

$$\begin{array}{r}3\\-1\\\hline 2\end{array}$$

$$\begin{array}{r}2\\-2\\\hline 1\end{array}$$

Junior Jugglers

Press **Questron** on the correct answer boxes.

Jan juggled **8**.

She dropped **2**.

How many are left?

| 6 | 7 | 8 |

Jay juggled **10**.

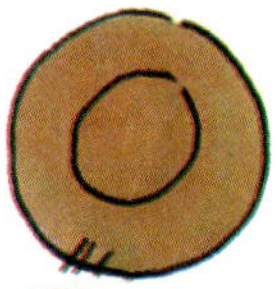

He dropped **4**.

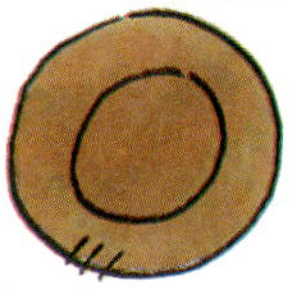

How many are left?

| 4 | 5 | 6 |

Jim juggled **6**.

He dropped **2**.

How many are left?

| 3 | 4 | 5 |

Jean juggled **7**.

She dropped **3**.

How many are left?

| 3 | 4 | 5 |

26

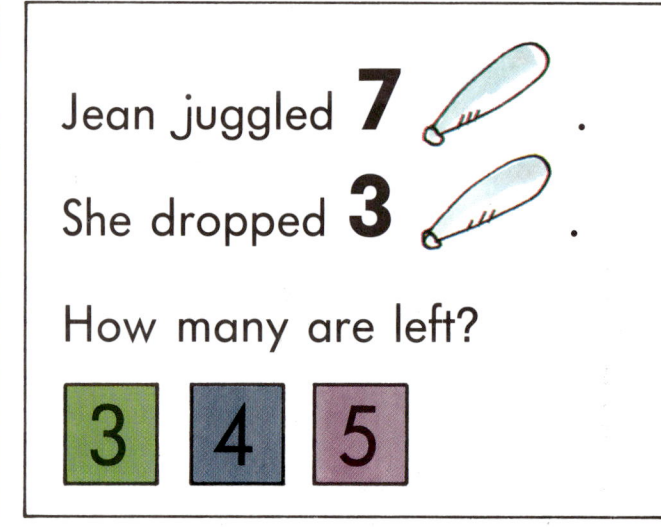

Skill: Solving word problems with subtraction

Jerry juggled **3** 🟠.

He dropped **1** 🟠.

How many are left?

| 1 | 2 | 3 |

Joan juggled **4** ⚪.

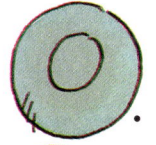

She dropped **0** ⚪.

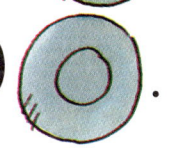

How many are left?

| 0 | 2 | 4 |

Jenny juggled **9** 🟡.

She dropped **1** 🟡.

How many are left?

| 8 | 9 | 10 |

Jack juggled **5** 🟢.

He dropped **1** 🟢.

How many are left?

| 2 | 3 | 4 |

Bus Stop

Track **Questron** on the path that has the correct answers. Start on the ☆.

$$\begin{array}{r}10\\-1\\\hline 8\end{array}$$

$$\begin{array}{r}10\\-1\\\hline 9\end{array}$$

$$\begin{array}{r}9\\-2\\\hline 6\end{array}$$

$$\begin{array}{r}9\\-2\\\hline 7\end{array}$$

$$\begin{array}{r}7\\-2\\\hline 5\end{array}$$

$$\begin{array}{r}7\\-2\\\hline 6\end{array}$$

Skill: Solving subtraction problems

$-\dfrac{1}{0}$

$-\dfrac{1}{2}$

$-\dfrac{2}{2}$

$-\dfrac{2}{1}$

$-\dfrac{4}{2}$

$-\dfrac{4}{3}$

$-\dfrac{5}{3}$

$-\dfrac{5}{4}$

Taking Off

Track **Questron** on the correct path. Follow the instructions on each maze. Start on the ☆.

Subtract **1** each time.

8	7	10	8
1	6	7	0
5	5	9	1
8	4	3	2

Subtract **2** each time.

10	8	6	7
9	12	4	2
11	5	3	0
3	0	9	1

Subtract **2** each time.

9	7	5	3
8	9	4	1
1	0	6	4
10	6	3	2

Skill: Identifying subtraction facts — numbers 1 to 10

Through the Clouds

Track **Questron** on the problems that have correct answers. Start on the ☆.

☆						
8−5=3	2−2=0	2−0=0	5−5=1	6−5=1	8−4=4	9−1=8
8−3=4	9−4=5	10−4=5	5−0=5	7−4=3	6−6=6	8−7=1
3−2=1	6−0=6	10−2=7	10−8=2	4−1=2	9−7=3	1−1=0
1−0=1	5−2=2	8−4=5	9−3=6	9−5=5	10−9=2	4−2=2
10−7=3	10−5=5	7−6=2	7−2=5	5−1=3	7−5=2	9−9=0
6−4=3	4−1=3	3−3=1	10−2=8	10−4=5	10−2=8	7−1=5
9−0=0	5−3=2	5−2=3	6−3=3	9−8=2	10−10=0	6−2=4

Skill: Identifying correct subtraction problems

31

THE QUESTRON LIBRARY OF ELECTRONIC BOOKS

A series of books specially designed to
reach — and teach — and entertain children of all ages

QUESTRON ELECTRONIC WORKBOOKS

Early Childhood	Grades K-5
My First Counting Book	My First Reading Book (K-1)
My First ABC Book	My First Book of Telling Time (1-3)
My First Book of Animals	Day of the Dinosaur (K-3)
Shapes and Sizes	First Grade Skills (1)
Preschool Skills	My First Book of Addition (1-2)
My First Vocabulary	The Storytime Activity Book (1-3)
My First Nursery Rhymes	My Robot Book (1-3)
Autos, Ships, Trains and Planes	My First Book of Spelling (1-3)
Reading Readiness	My First Book of Subtraction (1-3)
My First Words	My First Book of Multiplication (2-3)
My First Numbers	I Want to Be... (2-5)
Going Places	Number Fun (2-5)
Kindergarten Skills	Word Fun (2-5)

ELECTRONIC QUIZBOOKS FOR THE WHOLE FAMILY

Trivia Fun and Games
How, Why, Where and When
More How, Why, Where and When
World Records and Amazing Facts

PRICE/STERN/SLOAN — **RANDOM HOUSE, INC.**
Publishers, Inc., Los Angeles   *New York*